DECISIONS THAT SHAPE
SUPPLY CHAINS

CONSUMER CORNER SERIES
UNCONVENTIONAL LESSONS FROM CONSUMER BEHAVIOR

Why do consumers make the choices they do, and what can those choices teach us? The Consumer Corner series explores the subtle forces that shape consumer behavior, across topics that range from food, retail, health, vacations, and more. By spotlighting overlooked, counterintuitive, or nontraditional insights, the series challenges standard economic thinking and highlights the messy, human side of decision-making that sometimes occurs when humans engage in the marketplace. Drawing on behavioral science, lived experiences, and industry expertise, this series reveals what people can teach us as they make complex choices across the supply chain.

SERIES EDITOR

Nicole J. Olynk Widmar, Department Head and Professor of Agricultural Economics
Purdue University

DECISIONS THAT SHAPE SUPPLY CHAINS

NICOLE J. OLYNK WIDMAR
MICHAEL L. SMITH
ERIN ROBINSON

Purdue University Press
West Lafayette, Indiana

978-1-62671-230-0 (paperback)
978-1-62671-235-5 (epub)
978-1-62671-212-6 (epdf)

Cover image: Road through green pastures and trees, fork in the road: Yarphoto/iStock via Getty Images Plus.

CONTENTS

INTRODUCTION

Traditionally business management is rather, well, traditional. Some may even say stuffy. Of course, we didn't say that. We just pointed out that some people may have said that. Other people; not us. The reality is that running a business requires a diverse set of skills, like accounting, financial management, procurement, communication, strategic planning, project management, marketing, leadership, and time management. And that's before considering the expertise needed to actually perform the business's core function. In our industries, that means agricultural and food industry professionals, whether on-farm professionals making planting, fertilization, or investment decisions or food industry innovators bringing us safe and convenient ways to meet diverse nutritional needs.

The food system is diverse and complex, with businesses serving a variety of needs from transportation to storage, from field to production to processing, from marketing to packaging—the list goes on. There are many points of debate, from what crop to plant to which apple variety will be in demand three, five, or ten years from now. Regardless, one aspect of all businesses is universal: At the core of every decision is a person making it.

We get bogged down in classifying decisions—strategic versus tactical. This is actually an important distinction, because we need to prioritize and allocate time and effort accordingly. I mean, even the decision about how to allocate time to decisions is yet another decision. What to wear, what to eat for breakfast, which way to go to work, and whether to go out to dinner after work or go straight home to cook (and then what to cook). We make countless decisions every day, and decision fatigue is a legitimate problem. But do we acknowledge the threat and alter our behaviors to avoid fatigue and the perils that come along with it? We know celebrities, C-suite executives, and world leaders who adopt a daily structure as a means to reduce decision fatigue. Some people develop weekly dinner menus, ensuring that there's no need to decide what's for dinner when Monday rolls around—it's chicken and rice. If we fail to recognize how decision fatigue affects the quality of our choices, we might not ever adopt the structures, schedules, or frameworks to lessen its impact. Then again, even the decision to adopt a decision-limiting behavior is indeed another decision. Granted, it is one you make only once instead of daily, but it's still a decision.

There are a lot of frameworks and tools available to improve our decision-making. For starters, we can acknowledge that nearly every decision we make is a decision made under risk or with uncertainty. In classroom exercises, we often pretend that certainty exists—that if we do X, we will get Y. But in reality, if we do X, there is some probability that we will get Y, and some probability that we will get Z for any variety of reasons outside of our control. We control whether to take action X, but we don't control the weather, customer demand, or the fact that a competitor may have just invented a competing product that is simply better than ours. There are entire genres of business management books devoted to decision-making under risk or decision-making under uncertainty. This is important, and many of the tools to incorporate uncertainty into decision-making are among the more useful tools out there. Let's stop pretending there is some other category of decisions in which all outcomes are known with certainty. Perhaps, in limited cases, certainty can be assured. Realistically speaking, nearly every decision is made under risk. I think we would be better off to explicitly account for that—or at least acknowledge it even if we are not going to account for it.

One of the fascinating things about people making decisions is that we do it all the time, and yet most of us invest surprisingly little in the process of doing it. We invest even less in a process to evaluate how good or bad they were. We tend to evaluate decisions based on outcomes—many of which we cannot control—rather than assessing the quality of the decision itself. Many people fail to recognize that decision-making should follow a structured process or a framework, and those who do often only consider it within the context of business.

But what about those many other decisions we make when we're operating as consumers? Today, you may have decided what to buy for lunch, what to buy when grocery shopping, how and where to allocate household funds, or whether to make an investment (and, if so, which one). And that's just financial decisions. What about the scarcest resource of all—your time? Every day, you make choices about how you spend, or let's say invest, your time, hoping for some kind of return. The decision and its outcome are one thing, but how you arrived at that decision may be even more important.

There's so much to explore about how we make decisions. Most of what we tackle is mundane stuff you've seen before. But did you really stop to think about it? You almost certainly did not. Because decisions need to be made, and someone (you) has to make them. Throughout this book, we're pausing to consider what lessons we can draw from nontraditional places. We will talking about lessons from agriculture and food industries, but also unexpected places, and considering lessons from everyday consumer decisions. Be prepared to get outside of the box and think differently about your everyday life. Some ideas you take for granted—like "everyone loves Mickey Mouse"—may take on an entire new meaning when you look at them through the lens of decision-making and management.

There's plenty we already know but might not have considered deeply enough to shed light on our own decision-making within our professions. We know Mickey Mouse is beloved and an economic gold mine—but he's still a rodent. But have you ever considered why Mickey wears gloves? Because he represents all the good parts of a mouse and none of the bad. How many of our own businesses have less attractive features or aspects, and how are we managing those? How do we present only the best aspects of our business while managing the less attractive but necessary components?

While we argue that the agricultural and food supply chains can learn from consumer behavior and research, we also need to realize what is merely "interesting" or "nice to know" and what is truly actionable. Managing scarce resources, including time and attention, requires management skills and decision-making frameworks that can be assessed and refined.

This exploration of decision-making and management challenges us to reconsider our processes—or, if we're being honest, to acknowledge that we may not have defined a process at all. Have we avoided frameworks because they aren't necessary, or because adopting them would make us accountable for the outcomes? Ultimately, we're all making decisions every day. That's where we'll begin: with ourselves as consumers. After all, consumers are fickle, they're demanding, they're (seemingly) uninformed—they're you.

1

WHY IS A RAVEN LIKE A WRITING DESK?

I n Lewis Carroll's (1865) novel *Alice's Adventures in Wonderland*, the question "Why is a raven like a writing desk?" first appears.

QUESTION: Why is a raven like a writing desk?
ANSWER: A raven is not like a writing desk, and it doesn't matter why.

We human beings are inherently interested in riddles, solving problems, and finding solutions. Those most successful in your industry are the problem solvers. But was the problem they solved even worth solving? Does it actually matter?

Carroll proposed an answer to the riddle "Why is a raven like a writing desk?" in a preface to a later version of his work but openly admitted that no answer was originally intended. I am a devoted Alice fan as she has much to teach us about the perils and trials of sound decision-making. Spoiler alert: Consuming one mushroom in the forest with undesirable outcomes might make one pause before assuming that the solution to the next challenge is simply a different mushroom. To get to the heart of the matter: How much time is wasted answering questions for which there are no answers? And worse, how much time and effort do we spend celebrating ourselves or others for having answered them?

Particularly in the agricultural industries, where consumers feel disconnected from the fields and grain-handling facilities that supply their supermarkets and restaurants, we often ask questions that may not have clear answers. More fundamentally, is the question the right one, and does it even matter?

What are the most pertinent questions for your business in the realm of understanding consumers? Spending time, money, and energy determining why truck buyers don't pay a premium for bubblegum-pink trucks (or that mint-green shade Dodge attempted back in the late 1990s) seems unnecessary when one could simply paint trucks a color that consumers actually desire. Spending time, money, and energy determining why consumers are concerned about GMO use in food systems facilitates progress in feeding a growing population while using fewer chemicals on our fields. Thus, gaining a deeper understanding of consumer demand for products with and without GMO technology seems likely to yield a positive return on investment. In the heat of the moment and faced with our own dollars (and egos) at stake, it becomes difficult to discern which of the above two situations we are facing.

While I posit there is much the agricultural supply chains can learn from consumer demand and understanding consumer perceptions, we need to realize what is interesting or nice to know versus what is actionable. Without this knowledge, one risks wasting time and money answering question like, "Why is a raven like a writing desk?"

WORK CITED

Carroll, Lewis. 1865. *Alice's Adventures in Wonderland*. Macmillan.

_____

Adapted from original posting as *ConsumerCorner.2020.Letter.02.* (https://agribusiness.purdue.edu/consumer_corner/why-is-a-raven -like-a-writing-desk/)

2

STRAIGHT TALK ABOUT CONSUMER BEHAVIOR UNDER DURESS

On a personal note, parents are interesting human creatures, aren't they? One day you're eating food with a fork, maybe even while sitting down. The next thing you know, you're eating questionable leftovers while leaning over the sink (if you're lucky), without a fork in sight. (You lost all the forks? How?) Speaking only for myself: When did I become this confused, uncertain, hypocritical, yet incredibly demanding, unrecognizable version of myself? Thinking back to my infant parenting years, I was incredibly certain of what I wanted for my baby (sort of . . . maybe . . . actually, I'm not sure), even though I didn't know why. I mean, babies need these things. Don't they?

As consumers, infant parents are quite literally a nightmare, and the marketing for baby products is epically impactful (not that you can remember). Maybe it was good marketing. Or maybe you were just scared, gave up that day, and ordered what you thought your baby needed on Amazon—twice. It doesn't matter; I've been there and done that. You might have even ended up with three of them and don't remember what they were. But you have three of everything in the attic now, so you must have needed it.

Lesson One: We, as consumers, change our minds and demand things irrationally, which is perfectly acceptable in a market sense—as long as we're paying them.

The customer is always right. Right? So why do you try to tell them otherwise? Telling people what they do and do not like about food is risky business. Yes, agriculture and food companies, I'm looking at you. Are you guilty of telling people what to do, what to like, and how to perceive instead of meeting their demands as stated? Are you sure this is how you want to be remembered right now?

Lesson Two: We consumers remember if you offended us or made us feel bad for any of our unsavory consumer demands or behaviors. Bluntly stated, consumers under duress remember if you offended them.

There are two prominent, societally relevant examples of situations that cause stress, worry, fear, and some interesting consumer behaviors. Specifically, consider parenting and COVID-19 (or, for a real life-changing situation, consider both happening together). People facing stress and fatigue are not usually asking you for an education—they're asking for a product, an answer, or a solution they feel good about. Do you want to sell that to them or not? If you don't, that's fine. It is entirely conceivable that your company is uncomfortable producing or selling a certain product, service, or solution; is opposed to a production practice or technology; or simply cannot provide what is demanded in the necessary location or time. But don't feel compelled to give them something else for free, like advice, an education, or a lecture. The consumer may not be correct, but you have to decide if you want to tell them so—right here, right now—or if you want to have the chance to interact as trusted market players again another day.

Lesson Three: They say elephants never forget, but an elephant has nothing on a scared or stressed consumer's memory of whether (insert company or brand name here) made them feel worse instead of better.

New parents are a good example of a high-stress time in which they're likely not receptive to information counter to their own views. COVID-19 may have offered another situation in which people under stress are not looking to have an intellectually stimulating or even vaguely informational interaction with you. Know what you are trying to do out there in the marketplace, and be careful that you stray off that path with intention and not a misguided attempt to change someone's mind at the wrong time.

From the consumer and human standpoint, we can sympathize, and most of us have been there as the stressed-out consumer who just needs help finding whatever it is that they need (whether they need it or not, which isn't for you to weigh in on). What's the takeaway from a management lesson perspective specific to agricultural and food industries?

I am not proposing that you cannot seek to inform, provide transparency, or answer questions posed in the market. I am proposing that you stray off your core path of value creation with great care, thought, and planning and be considerate of the state of your consumer. Consumers under duress are looking for safety, certainty, and help. There is an inherent trust being placed in product and service providers during uncertain times. Consider the reliance on grocery stores during COVID-19: Consumers placed great trust in those retailers to provide food for their families during uncertain times. Grocery stores became celebrated beacons of comfort, even as the experience inside was nerve-wracking for many. People wanted help feeding their families and many had no capacity for conversations about food, nutrition, or the production practices of various products. They needed food for their kids—now! It simply wasn't the time for information or education, regardless of how well intentioned. Remember what they came to you for, and consider carefully whether this is the time for care, compassion, and answering only the request being placed versus providing more than was asked for at a time when people may not be equipped to handle more information than requested.

Lesson Four: If people are coming to you for products, services, or solutions under duress, you have been given an implicit trust—treat that with great care. Pardon my language, but "Hell hath no fury like a stressed-out consumer scorned."

––––––––––

Adapted from original posting as *ConsumerCorner.2020.Letter.07.* (https://agribusiness.purdue.edu/consumer_corner/straight-talk-about
-consumer-behavior-under-duress/)

3

YOU ARE SUCH
A HYPOCRITE!

Y ou are such a hypocrite!" or the equally prickly stereotypical version, "They are such hypocrites!" are retorts that get flung around quite often in debates about natural resource use and the environment. Increasingly, these phrases are also used in production agriculture where natural resource use intersects with the production of goods for human consumption in perhaps the most obvious and spectacular way. In addition to being an insult, or at least seemingly intended as one, it makes for an excellent starting point in an argument because, well, it is true! The problem is that if you stop to look in a mirror, it turns out the comeback, "And so are you!" is equally true. When it comes to consumption (which we all do) and consumers (which we all are), we are indeed all hypocrites.

Unfortunately, this universal truth-turned-insult gets us nowhere except embroiled in an us-versus-them debate between producers and consumers. This debate and inability, or unwillingness, to listen and hear one another without pre-forming our explanation of why we are right has gotten us where we are now. You cannot engage in battle with your consumer and expect to come out ahead; it simply does not work. In short bursts, it may seem to work when businesses and corporations get their way, but building resentment with your customer is seldom a long-term path to success.

> Actions that directly violate our stated priorities run rampant, and this is particularly true around matters of environmentalism. You could argue it's impossible to even live normally in some form of shelter with some form of energy for heat, light, or transportation and not create negative impacts on the environment. Simply living could contradict a stated intention to care for and prioritize (or even want to save) the environment. (Vincent et al. 2017, 138)

In 2016, I began a journey of co-authoring a book, which has become one of my proudest accomplishments. Together, a third-generation logger from Libby, Montana (Bruce Vincent), a professor (yours truly), and a writer/author/communications expert (Jessica Eise) embarked on a journey to give "a powerful firsthand account of life in rural America that offers a broad, probing look at the environmental tension surrounding the collapse of many of our rural resource communities" (Vincent et al. 2017, back cover).

The result of our collaboration is the heart-wrenching story of Vincent Logging and the annotated life story of Bruce Vincent, told in 169 pages of text. More personally, the result is a stronger understanding of what I seek as my own contribution to the world with respect to my research and educational outreach efforts—to aid agricultural and natural resource–intensive industries in how to navigate production decisions while taking into account the demands and perspectives of the human beings who inhabit this earth and thus have a stake in those resources, even if they do not have any interest in purchasing or partaking in what you are producing.

Hypocrisy creates significant communication barriers, and none of us are immune. Everyday mundane activities reveal us as hypocritical, as our stated beliefs collide with our personal actions and our own budgetary constraints. Examples include donating to charities to offset other expenditures for which we feel guilt, wastefulness, or even inappropriate, or a stated devotion to reduction in greenhouse gas emission followed by heating one's home, consuming electricity, driving a car (or SUV!), and taking vacations to faraway places reached by airplane.

A little closer to home for agribusinesses are the food and fiber industries and the processes employed in the production of the products that feed, house, and clothe us all. Animal agriculture is rich with opportunities for hypocrisy. Farm landscapes and farm animals are ubiquitous in children's stories. Relatability to animals is cultivated almost from birth, whether children are born into rural, urban, or suburban childhoods. Yet, those farm animals we feature in cartoons, stuffed toys, and coloring books are the same ones we eat.

> Bears, cats, mice and a whole lot of talking, feeling and emotion-laden farm animals have warmed our hearts for generations. Yet, many of the stars of such media are also features of the dinner table. They are our beloved friends and heroes on one hand, but on the other? Most of us don't have even a second thought of serving them up for dinner. (Vincent et al. 2017, 141)

Hypocrisy is all around us; we each participate fully whether we have framed it as such or not. Production of food, like production of any goods, is a balancing act of tradeoffs between the products we get (goods) and the negative externalities that we create as by-products. Most of the strife and argument between producers and consumers in animal agriculture today, and agricultural production systems more broadly, revolve around the tradeoffs. Fundamentally, the argument is around the question, "What is an acceptable tradeoff?"

Yet, my friend Bruce Vincent said it best: "We can't keep using the hypocrisy of others as a veil for why we shouldn't seek to do anything productive. Positive actions are positive and they should be encouraged out of our internal drive or moral obligations. Even though we, or they, are likely still hypocrites anyway" (Vincent et al. 2017, 141).

WORK CITED

Vincent, Bruce, Nicole J. Olynk Widmar, and Jessica Eise. 2017. *Against the Odds: A Path Forward for Rural America.* CreateSpace Independent Publishing Platform.

———————

Adapted from original posting as *ConsumerCorner.2020.Letter.08.* (https://agribusiness.purdue.edu/consumer_corner/you-are-such-a -hypocrite/)

4

WHY REVERED RODENTS WEAR GLOVES

Inspired by and quotes taken from Against the Odds: A Path Forward for Rural America *(Vincent et al. 2017).*

I t is impossible to ignore that animal agriculture provides a (virtual) gateway into agriculture for people otherwise not exposed. Animals are inherently relatable, even to young children, who connect with them through stuffed cows and pigs and coloring books full of farm scenes reminiscent of *Old MacDonald's Farm*. If that still feels too distant, the beloved farm dog depicted in that storybook looks an awful lot like Lassie, doesn't he? Nearly every child has a stuffed animal in their bed, but very, very few have a stuffed corn kernel or soybean to clutch tightly. (We're big fans of the field crops; if corn kernels were accessible as stuffed toys, I'm certain our child would have one. But they aren't available and aren't even called stuffed toys. They are called stuffed animals.)

This relatability to animals, despite possibly never having met that animal face-to-face, begins very early in life. Many children possess at least one, or many more than one, stuffed animals of some kind. But very few children are found sleeping with their cherished stuffed soybean. Beloved classics such as *Charlotte's Web* (1952) and *Stuart Little* by E. B. White (1945) introduce children to animals as their friends and confidants. Animals in media are often presented as children's friends and protectors. They are frequently defined as fiercely loyal, genuinely kind and with positive emotional appeal. One cannot forget the various dangerous situations which Lassie (the fictional dog character created by Eric Knight who starred in her own 1954 television series) and Flipper, the beloved television star bottlenose dolphin, traversed to help the children in their care.

The Cat in the Hat by Dr. Seuss is famous the world over. He has carried decades of children (and adults, perhaps) through adventures in books, and even on television. The book *Winnie-the-Pooh* by A. A. Milne (1926) has inspired much attention. Winnie-the-Pooh, along with his pals from the Hundred-Acre-Wood, have been friends to children since 1926. Pooh Bear, as his friends call him, is prominently featured in books, plush toys, clothing and on video. Perhaps the most undisputable evidence of Pooh Bear's fame is that the rights to Winnie-the-Pooh were licensed to Walt Disney Productions. Pooh Bear and his friends remain the feature characters at The Crystal Palace in Magic Kingdom at Walt Disney World Resort in Orlando, Florida, a testament to their fame and prominence in popular culture (and perceived economic potential). (Vincent et al. 2017, 140)

Perhaps you are now convinced that animals are agriculture's gateway to conversation with the public. Now, we switch gears to examine animals and society more generally, moving outside the agricultural links. I want to point to a rodent—the mouse—for further consideration. In particular, I present the curious case of revered rodents.

Consider the peculiar case of revered rodents. We cherish memories of our first read of *Stuart Little*. And who among us does not love the internationally recognized poster-mouse of family fun and childhood wonder (and perhaps even magic), Mickey Mouse? So love Mickey Mouse, but now go set traps for the mouse (likely not a famous mouse, but a mouse nonetheless) in your house. (Vincent et al. 2017, 140)

As a reminder from chapter 3, you are most certainly a hypocrite. One mouse you hug and one mouse you poison, glue to sticky paper, and unceremoniously crush to rid your house of vermin. What makes Mickey Mouse palatable and epically famous? Well, for starters, he embodies all the good parts of a mouse and none of the bad. He's furry (good), he's got adorable whiskers (good), he's generally cuddly (good), and he's as smiley as a mouse can smile (good). Rodent features that are less attractive might include rodent teeth and rodent paws. Mickey has neither. He's curiously lacking prominent rodent teeth (I have no explanation, so we'll accept that at face value), but hugs from Mickey Mouse are the things of childhood dreams. Being hugged by rodent paws with their little scratchy nails (those same little nails you hear scratching in your walls) is not attractive. Hence, the big white gloves. Mickey Mouse is always wearing his gloves. It's likely you have not put much thought into Mickey's gloves prior to now, so allow me to provide my own personally collected evidence.

At this point, you may be concerned that we've ventured off course in deriving consumer insights for agriculture and food, but I assure you the gloves on this revered rodent are providing a relevant lesson. Even Mickey Mouse has some unattractive characteristics. He's beloved, he's revered, he's a childhood dream, he's an economic gold mine— but he's still a rodent with little rodent paws that we cover up with big white gloves.

Every production system in the world, every society, every aspect of life as we live it has details that are less than pleasant. We create trash, so we put it in scented bags (yes, you can perfume your trash) and take it outside to a trash can that will hide the trash bags (double points given if your trash can is somehow decorated, a color that matches your house, or even has a little shelter of its own). Then, trash gets picked up and taken away. It disappears as if by magic. We pay, either privately or indirectly through government services, to be separated from the less-than-pleasant by-product of living—trash disposal. Trash is easy, and we can all agree that most people don't care for trash.

What about processing livestock animals into meat products? Meat processing plants are not generally thought to be the most pleasant environments. Kill floors, hanging carcasses, and cutting floors are unpalatable to many people, evidenced by the very few consumers who would sign up to process their own meat or wish to tour a kill floor. Generally speaking, we like our meat to come in reasonable container sizes, require minimal processing at home, and at times, we even pay for things like no-touch packaging. In other words, there are unpleasant aspects of turning livestock animals into meat products we are comfortable cooking at home. Thus, we pay others to do those things for us, separating ourselves from the unpleasant aspects we don't want to do, see, or be involved with. Fundamentally, we maintain access to the good aspects (meat for consumption) while distancing ourselves from the negative aspects (slaughter). In other words, we're keeping the gloves on—putting the negatives out of sight while maintaining access to the positives.

Transparency and honesty are good, but forcing uncomfortable truths onto unsuspecting individuals might not be. Separating oneself from animal slaughter, hiding trash storage and disposal, and covering up rodent paws are all essentially the same behaviors. We limit exposure to the bad while maintaining access to the good by using the market—paying others to do the things we don't enjoy or wish to be involved with.

Forcing consumers to confront uncomfortable truths like the process of slaughter is essentially ripping off Mickey's glove to reveal the rodent paw underneath. If consumers are asking questions, then providing access to truthful information is the right response. But how often do we seek to demonstrate processes in the name of transparency or proof that what we do is hard, complicated, or unpleasant only to risk alienating people? I remain in favor of telling the truth about what we do in agricultural production; however, it may be worth thinking about whether we sometimes overexpose information to make a point. Answer calls for transparency, but be careful not to rip off Mickey's glove without warning, or without sensitivity to how your message may be perceived.

WORKS CITED

Milne, A. A. 1926. *Winnie the Pooh*. Methuen.

Seuss, Dr. 1957. *The Cat in the Hat*. Random House, Houghton Mifflin.

Vincent, Bruce, Nicole J. Olynk Widmar, and Jessica Eise. 2017. *Against the Odds: A Path Forward for Rural America*. CreateSpace Independent Publishing Platform.

White, E. B. 1945. *Stuart Little*. Harper & Brothers.

White, E. B. 1952. *Charlotte's Web*. Harper & Brothers.

Adapted from original posting as *ConsumerCorner.2020.Letter.09*. (https://agribusiness.purdue.edu/consumer_corner/why-revered-rodents -wear-gloves/)

5

NO OFFENSE, BUT . . .

I have spent most of my career attempting to understand what consumers want from production agriculture. I've also worked to foster dialogue among individuals holding differing perspectives on matters such as production methods, animal welfare, and other contentious topics. I've come to loathe common phrases used in discussions regarding costs and benefits of production agriculture and food systems, the first of which is, "No offense, but . . ." and the worst, "With all due respect . . ."

It doesn't matter what follows those three little words—"No offense, but . . ."—it instantly puts the receiver on edge. Why not just go ahead and admit, "I'm gearing up to unleash some offensiveness, but let's pretend I'm being polite by giving you this heads-up that nobody asked for." Isn't it delightful how you're not only dishing out the offense but also proudly broadcasting that you're fully aware of it?

Fundamentally, you've just shifted the burden of your statement to the recipient. If they feel offended by your statement, it's on them. Probably not the best strategy if your intention is to make the recipient of your words actually want to communicate with you. Rest assured, "No offense, but . . ." isn't the only statement of this kind that gets under my skin:

- Appears harmless, but conceals a sting: No offense, but . . .
- A similar sentiment for the less subtle: Don't be offended, but . . .

- My personal favorite, master of mixed signals: With all due respect …

"With all due respect" is very seldom followed with respect, in my experience. Its mere utterance raises suspicion, as one might argue that if genuine respect were present, there'd be no need to announce it. What typically follows is a total lack of respect, implying that no respect was due at all. Ouch.

Whether you think some folks are overly sensitive or find my letter addressing the topic of offense itself offensive, one fact remains: Words matter. So, mind your manners. Connotation matters, too. In production agriculture and food industries, substantial resources are invested in comprehending the consumer's perspective, whether they choose to buy our products or not. If we truly want to understand what others think or feel, we should refrain from shutting down two-way communication with our opening statement.

"With all due respect, you haven't got a clue about what it takes to get food from farm to fork." "No offense, but that is not how the food system works."

The heart of matter may be true—most people not directly engaged in a particular production system lack comprehensive knowledge about it. But are those little introductory phrases truly necessary? Rarely so. Do they facilitate the free flow of ideas, thoughts, and beliefs? Almost certainly not. A simple cost-benefit analysis would determine that the cost of such phrases is reasonably high, and the benefit in most settings is near zero. Expecting someone whom you've just offended to engage in meaningful dialogue is unrealistic. So, if you're genuinely on the hunt for productive conversations, rather than one-sided soapbox speeches, just a little reminder: Words matter, and don't forget your manners.

Adapted from original posting as *ConsumerCorner.2023.Letter.20*. (https://agribusiness.purdue.edu/consumer_corner/no-offense-but -words-do-matter/)

6

IN FAVOR OF DIFFERENTIATION

BY MARIO ORTEZ

G rowing up with coffee growers, I learned to appreciate a regular cup of coffee (made with nondifferentiated commodity beans) at the dawn of a foggy morning on the farm. It wasn't until adulthood, when I owned a small coffee plantation, that I felt the need to train to be more of a coffee connoisseur. This training has been a great deal of fun, but it was fundamentally a strategic business decision. Differentiated specialty coffee production opens the door to differentiated sophisticated consumers in markets with high purchasing power. These consumers enjoy learning about what you do on the farm when it comes to harvesting and processing the beans that become the coffee they drink before work or share with friends.

I would bet that the shepherd who observed how excited his goats were after eating beans from coffee bushes in the Ethiopian highlands more than ten centuries ago (while we don't know if this is the true story behind the discovery of coffee, it sounded cool the first time I heard it) did not foresee today's vast and complex world of coffee—both commodity and specialty.

There seem to be consistent patterns in what consumers want, at least when it comes to specialty and differentiated foods. The usual requirements like affordability, safety, freshness, and taste still hold. But a more recent trend seems to be the desire for information: the story behind the product. Having lived in five different countries, including the United

FIGURE 6.1. I harvested the first beans of the 2019–2020 harvest.

States, I've found a common theme from rural Nicaraguan supermarkets all the way to downtown Chicago—people want to know where their food comes from.

Buying and selling goods are enhanced when consumers have complete, easily digestible, and readily accessible information about a product's origin and production methods. A true premium experience also includes details about the people behind the product. In some ways this storytelling is easier back in the little marketplace of northern Nicaragua, because we can just ask the merchants where their vegetables or grains came from, and most often, they grew and harvested them with their own hands. Here in the United States, unless you are at a farmer's market, this connection is hard to establish. Product labels, social media, and company websites help transfer this information from producer to consumer.

On our small farm, Los Cielitos (which means "the little skies"—a nod to its high elevation, where you often feel you're close to the sky), we provide information about our coffee's production and processing through product labels and the roaster's website. Consumers can learn about varieties like Catuai, the washing process (which happens right after harvest), roast level (medium, light, or dark), and cupping notes (the hints of flavor to expect in a cup).

One of the lessons we have learned from the market and applied to Los Cielitos is that having options, such as different varieties, roast levels, and grind levels, is something consumers appreciate. Why? Some genuinely prefer a specific blend, but many show appreciation because they have developed a taste for the art of brewing coffee. For example, if you use a French press, CHEMEX®, or an espresso maker, you will want different grind levels.

The idea of purchasing and developing Los Cielitos emerged from observing the growing market of specialty coffee. With our family's coffee growing expertise and our understanding of the challenges conventional coffee growers face in making a living, we saw an opportunity. By decreasing the number of intermediaries, we could connect coffee drinkers more directly with high-quality, specialty coffee.

Our business model was initially funded by my brother, my uncle, and me. My parents operate the farm on-site with the help of many people in the area. We strongly believe that being more strategic in the way we grow and sell agricultural goods in Nicaragua—similar to many developing countries where agriculture is central to livelihoods—can positively impact the overall welfare of local communities while enhancing the consumer's coffee experience.

From my roots in coffee farming, I had the chance to follow the traditional and well-worn path of producing conventional coffee. However, I found the specialty coffee market too compelling to pass up. In taking this route, I've accepted more risk for the chance of higher financial reward. Whether or not the differentiated coffee strategy will be successful, we have yet to see.

Adapted from original posting as *ConsumerCorner.2020.Letter.14*. (https://agribusiness.purdue.edu/consumer_corner/in-favor-or -differentiation/)

7

BUSINESS
DECISION-MAKING
AND PULLING
THE PLUG

Warren Buffett famously said (and has since repeated), "The most important thing to do if you find yourself in a hole is to stop digging." Sounds simple and makes good sense. The problem is that we don't listen. Alice (of *Alice's Adventures in Wonderland*, 1865) said it best, "I give myself very good advice, but I very seldom follow it. That explains the trouble that I'm always in."

But why can't we stop digging? We're all (seemingly) adults in business, and we got here by making decisions, sticking with them, and eventually persevering. Over our lifetimes and as we get further along in our careers, persevering seems to shift from something that looks like winning to simply being pleased about surviving a Wednesday afternoon and making it halfway through the work week. At what point did aiming for the top of the mountain peak morph into just making it through another day?

Admittedly, that was extreme. But the sentiment remains—why are we so afraid to pull the plug on projects, investments, and endeavors in business? Why can't we admit when we need to stop digging and start changing directions, ending a project, or discontinuing an investment activity?

Interestingly, children—those honest and outspoken creatures—do not suffer from the inability to stop digging. If children decide halfway through an activity that they no longer like it, they pull the plug and get out of there. Take a trip to meet the Easter Bunny as evidence. At first you're just a kid sitting on the lap of a bunny in the local mall, and it seems okay. The décor is questionable and you are secretly wondering what your parents are getting out of this experience, but so far, so good. You sit there (looking adorable) until you glance over your left shoulder and catch an up-close glimpse of this mall bunny character. Yup, that's a 1980s-style mall bunny. He's scary, and he smells a little funny too. So, naturally, you scream your baby head off and get the heck out of there. Why? Because you weren't afraid to reassess the situation, change your mind, and pull the plug on the whole operation.

So what's wrong with adults? Quite a few things. To name just a few:

- We lose track of what was intended to be permanent versus a trial in the first place (or we were never explicit up front on what is a forever commitment versus a "for right now" commitment).
- We overestimate the costs of stopping or fall victim to a variety of sunk cost fallacies.
- We have been repeatedly patted on the back for sticking it out in the past and we feel social pressure.
- We are afraid of the politics of wanting to reverse course on the decision of our predecessor or higher-ups.

Admittedly, I've mixed personal examples into my attempt to make the point that the ability and willingness to pull the plug on business and professional activities, initiatives, and investments is important and underappreciated. Interestingly, we tend to be a bit clearer in our personal lives in what is a long-term or forever commitment versus a short-term arrangement. We enter into marriage vows "until death do us part," making clear the commitment timeline. We buy homes with thirty-year mortgages, making clear the relatively weighty commitment, at least relative to a one-year apartment lease or one-week hotel stay. Seldom are we this deliberate in our intended timelines and investments professionally.

Professionally speaking, we can aid ourselves by being deliberate in our intended timelines and length of commitment. If a project is being undertaken as an experiment, then being deliberate in saying so and setting a timeline for evaluation is critical. Evaluation by decision makers not responsible for the initial project launch can help.

Much of the problem around pulling the plug is tied to us as human beings. If the project or investment lead manager has a job title that mimics the project's name, can you really expect that person to feel comfortable pulling the plug on that project if it is no longer the best use of company resources? Maybe, but it would take deliberate cultivation of culture, support systems, and safety nets for honest managers and decision-making frameworks to make that possible. Additionally, it would take even more effort and nurturing of culture to make it probable.

ACKNOWLEDGMENTS AND INSPIRATION

This Consumer Corner letter was inspired by Straw and Ross (March 1987) and ten years of co-teaching strategic decision making with Dr. Allan Gray and Dr. Michael Boehjle during which I was privileged to teach decision traps and pulling the plug.

WORKS CITED

Carroll, Lewis. 1865. *Alice's Adventures in Wonderland*. Macmillan.

Straw, Barry, and Jerry Ross. 1987. "Knowing When to Pull the Plug." *Harvard Business Review*. March. Accessed 2025. https://hbr.org/1987/03/knowing-when-to-pull-the-plug.

like production, but we don't like its consequences—at least not near us, where we have to experience them.

Bruce Vincent, Nicole J. Olynk Widmar, and Jessica Eise explain in *Against the Odds: A Path Forward for Rural America*:

> Not in my backyard, or aptly called NIMBY, is a commonly used term to express opposition to any undesired elements sitting near one's residence or new civic projects. For instance, individuals desire community services and amenities, such as garbage and recycling facilities. But NIMBY is a near universal desire to have that necessary amenity located away from your own residence. Although, of course, it should still be within a reasonable distance so it can provide your service in a convenient fashion.
>
> In other words, I want my garbage to be picked up and disposed of in an orderly and timely fashion, but I don't want to smell or see the garbage dump. And actually, while I'm at it, I prefer not to see too much truck traffic, especially not garbage trucks (which begs the question of how trash should be transported to the far away dump). Beyond the obvious need for some tradeoff in garbage dump location between close and far away, the more fatal flaw exists in the fact that the garbage dump (or jail or other less desirable item) needs to be located somewhere. And this means that it will be located near someone.
>
> Everyone can agree that a garbage dump is necessary and thus needs a location. In other cases, we can also all agree that a certain project is necessary and consequently needs to be located somewhere. We all remain fine with these universally accepted truths, so long as the location chosen is not in my backyard!
>
> Our urge to locate unpleasant facilities or those with negative impacts, such as odors, environmental challenges or unpleasing aesthetics, far away extends well beyond just civic projects. Think about any type of desired or necessary production. Then think about the location of that production. Or what about the land set aside from production, lands that are specifically protected? Perhaps these lands are protected from logging, hunting or are protected to preserve a habitat for animals which we, as a society, would like to see preserved or saved—but

our individual support for this protection evaporates if the land in question is used by us for a purpose disallowed by the proposed protection.

Saving bears sounds great. Enabling bears' reproduction so there is a larger population also sounds great, particularly if you feel an affinity towards wildlife and wish to see wildlife populations preserved. But where should those bears live? Do you want them to live in your backyard? Well, perhaps you would like to see them saved somewhere in North America, which seems close enough to be meaningful (in the spirit of claiming production close to home), but far enough away that they pose no danger to my dog in the backyard (or child for that matter).

So we desire goods, including the piles of plastics and consumer electronics. These goods are produced somewhere, and somewhere nearby that somewhere, there are residents facing the negative consequences of such production. Yet as the consumer of goods, how many of those negative consequences do you actually see? The answer depends on where you live. But given the vast diversity of products that most of us in society consume regularly, the response is likely "not many."

Therein lies the paradox of production. We want the goods, but we don't want them to be produced. More specifically, we don't want to incur the costs, largely nonmonetary, of their production. People in both urban and rural settings share similar reactions. It's just the same with our civic projects. We want them close enough to service our needs or desires but let's keep them far enough away so I don't suffer negative consequences of the byproducts of production, such as noise or stink, for example.

Factories can create smog, water pollution and traffic. Livestock operations can create water pollution or even truck traffic, not to mention the foul odors. By biological process, chickens, pigs, sheep, goats and cattle produce manure and excrement. But most of us like to eat our meat, thus necessitating livestock production and the existence of farms housing livestock animals. The existence, you say, is not the problem (for the majority of people), but it's the site selected. Simply allow the placement of such, potentially offensive, facilities away from me. Well, the problem is that "away from you" generally means nearer to someone else.

Local siting decisions are rather simple to imagine. Does the new livestock facility locate on this side of the mile section of ground or on the opposite side? Does the new plant locate north or south of the highway? Does a manufacturing plant locate within 1 mile or 10 miles of the new housing development? The conversation becomes more difficult when considering the global exchange of goods and global trade partners. If you want random plastic household goods, for argument's sake, but don't want the environmental impacts associated with production near your home, then the production facility may be forced to locate further away. What does further away mean in this case? Across state lines? In another country? The relocation of production does not eliminate the negative aspects of production. It just relocates them. (Vincent et al. 2017, 89)

The consequences of production harm others, whether air or water pollution from a factory or even noise or dust disturbing neighbors of farm fields. There are also consequences of production that serve others positively, such as amenities like wildlife animal habitats (for those who value having wildlife around) or scenic views. In the case of scenic views, there are boutique hotels and resorts that profit from distant views of black and white cows dotting green pastures. More commonly, though, we think of the negatives—from smells to noise to pollution—that affect those close to production facilities, whether they are consumers of the goods produced or not.

WORK CITED

Vincent, Bruce, Nicole J. Olynk Widmar, and Jessica Eise. 2017. *Against the Odds: A Path Forward for Rural America.* CreateSpace Independent Publishing Platform.

Adapted from original posting as *ConsumerCorner.2020.Letter.21.* (https://agribusiness.purdue.edu/consumer_corner/revisiting-the -production-paradox/)

9

THOUGHTS ON VALUE, COST, AND PRICE

BY MARIO ORTEZ

Value and price have been a matter of discussion for moral philosophers and economics writers ever since antiquity. For example, see the thoughts of Aristotle and St. Thomas Aquinas on fairness, price, value, trade, buyers, and sellers. Economic historian Raymond de Roover summarized the historically prominent trends of thought when regarding value determination: Either value depends upon the perceived utility by individuals, or value is created by the labor or cost incorporated in exchangeable goods.

The articulation of a value theory based on subjective utility is credited to Pierre de Jean Olivi, O.F.M. (1248–1298). Building upon Olivi's earlier work, San Bernardino of Sienna, O.F.M. (1380–1444) stated that value is composed of three elements: usefulness, scarcity, and pleasurableness or desirability. In his magnum opus, *History of Economic Analysis* (1954), Joseph Schumpeter (1883–1950), one of the most influential economists of the early twentieth century, praised the work of these friars "for ascribing a comprehensive vision to the economic process." To be fair, a famous exponent of the second idea that cost (which labor is part of) creates value is the Marxian system, taking after the famous German polymath Karl Marx (1818–1883), according to which the quantity of labor alone creates value.

But that is enough history for now, and I presume you have now been convinced by history and philosophical inquiry that price does not (or may not, if you wish to be cautious) equal cost—if you weren't already of this opinion before.

As a coffee farmer myself, the concept of cost is straightforward. I invest in technology and better inputs not for the sake of good-looking coffee bushes (though this may be fulfilling), but expecting an economic return on my investment. Whether or not I earn a return is dependent upon what the market demands. In other words, is my coffee going to generate extra utility for the beholder? If it is, has that extra utility generated enough to justify my added costs? The dichotomy happens when you go about your business adding inputs and practices and simply expecting compensation without regard to whether the market wants them.

Let me explain what I mean in a different way: A consumer at the store probably does not see a bag of organic coffee and wonder how much it cost to produce it; instead, they may wonder how much they might increase their own utility or happiness by buying organic, for whatever reason it makes them as an individual happier. To the organic coffee drinker, the cost to the farm to produce the product is entirely irrelevant. Speaking again about the coffee drinker, the price of the product and its value (or expected utility) are relevant but not driven by production cost.

It's about supply and demand, not cost to produce. In the coffee world, the international coffee price is the result of the interaction between global supply and global demand. Global demand is largely impacted by consumer trends, which, in turn, are influenced by cultural views of the drink, availability of substitute products, and such factors.

Speaking of the global influence of a single product, coffee was credited with fueling the ensuing scientific and financial revolutions of the seventeenth century. It is indeed a big deal. Global supply is affected by factors such as droughts in major producing countries or when a new country like Vietnam (which used to produce no coffee thirty years ago and is now ranked among the top five producers in the world) enters the market. The recent dips in coffee prices are largely credited to a few years of surplus from Brazil, the world's largest coffee producer. My main point here is that the value of this good is not given by the cost incurred in producing it, but by a wide array of economic forces driven by coffee's usefulness, scarcity, and pleasurableness or desirability—just as San Bernardino formalized.

I experienced these concepts of cost and value in a different way when I worked pricing meat here in the United States. At times, I observed how the price for meat at my neighborhood store was considerably lower than what the store had paid the packer for the same product. Instead of the typical 60-pound box at the wholesale level, the store would have a tray with one to several steaks, but beyond breaking a big package into smaller ones, no additional value was added. Why was this?

Certainly, food retailers in this country were not making a mistake; they knew the wholesale price they paid but were willing to sell it at a lower price to the end consumer. I came to learn that driving people to their store with weekly ads had far more value for the store than losses generated by setting the selling price for this item (beef) under their cost. Store traffic is valuable! When I go to the store to get a steak, I also get potatoes, salad items, and maybe some locally brewed beers. The customer's bundle generates dollars in margin that more than make up for the loss on the steak today (and pork tomorrow, and so on). Regardless, the cost did not determine the price in the retail setting, nor the value of the product.

What is the ultimate message here? Keep your investments aligned with market demands. The cost you incur in producing a good is key to your financial success, but don't get confused along the way. Your target market absolutely does not care about how much it cost you to provide it when they decide how much they are willing to pay for your product.

WORKS CITED

Economist. 2020. "The Story of Coffee Is a Parable of Global Capitalism." April 23. *The Economist*. Retrieved from https://www.economist.com/books-and-arts/2020/04/23/the-story-of-coffee-is-a-parable-of-global-capitalism.

Prasad, R. 2019. *How the 2019 Coffee Crisis Might Affect You*. July 11. Retrieved from BBC.com: https://www.bbc.com/news/world-us-canada-48631129.

Roover, R. D. 1950–1963. *Saint Bernardino of Siena*. Opera omnia. 8 vols.

Roover, R. D. 1967. *San Bernardino of Siena and Sant'Antonino of Florence: The Two Great Economic Thinkers of the Middle Ages.* Kress Library of Business and Economics, Harvard Graduate School of Business Administration.

Schumpeter, J. 1954. *History of Economic Analysis.* Oxford University Press.

Adapted from original posting as *ConsumerCorner.2020.Letter.26.* (https://agribusiness.purdue.edu/consumer_corner/thoughts-on-value-cost-and-price/)

10

WHY ARE YOU COMPLAINING?

(Is This a Sport? Are You Trying to Win a Medal?)

W e all dread being on the receiving end of complaints. Complaints are inherently bad; it's in the definition. From Dictionary.com, a complaint is "an expression of discontent, regret, pain, censure, resentment, or grief; lament; faultfinding." Use it in a sentence and what comes to mind? "I plan to lodge a formal complaint."

But why? Why are you lodging a formal complaint? Why are you complaining?

Perhaps you are indeed looking for a situation to be remedied. In that case, you are seeking a change or solution. If you seek a remedy, as in, you got a sandwich with mayo when you specifically asked for one without (because you do not like even being in the same general vicinity as mayo), then wouldn't it be more accurate to say that you are going to ask for the correct sandwich? You could choose to complain, whine, and yell at someone about your mayo intolerance having been violated, or, if you actually sought a sandwich without mayo, you could simply ask for that directly and skip the berating of the person who incorrectly served it to you. This could be called remedying a situation, correcting a mistake, or seeking an alternative action or item.

Alternatively, maybe you want something you cannot have. You may want an airplane to fly to Minneapolis in a snowstorm tonight—preferably right now, at this very second. However, it has been determined by someone other than the gate agent standing in front of you that the airplane you see will not be flying to Minneapolis in a snowstorm tonight, and neither will you. We've all witnessed it and maybe even been there a time or two ourselves—the airport-induced adult version of the hissy fit that these situations tend to bring out. And although the lack of flying taking place isn't the gate agent's fault, they are likely to feel the unleashed wrath of said hissy fit.

But why? What is the goal in complaining to the gate agent who almost certainly does not control the fate of this aircraft tonight (or on any other night)? Why are you complaining?

Will yelling at, pointing at, or otherwise expressing your discontent at the gate agent make the plane fly? What will expressing your discontent, pain, regret, or resentment get you? Not onto the airplane and into the air, that's for sure. Yes, it might get you connected to someone higher up or in customer service to try to make you stop complaining, perhaps by offering you a token gift of miles or a better seat when the snowstorm lets up tomorrow. But is that what you wanted? I thought you wanted to fly to Minneapolis, which you did not do regardless.

Perhaps you are seeking some form of restitution. You want miles, a hotel room, or an apology. Indeed, you may be entitled to such things, assuming you have not yet embarrassed yourself in a YouTube-worthy scene. But complaining is highly unlikely to be the only path forward here. And it is seldom going to be the most pleasant path forward for the complainer or the complainee. You could ask for a hotel room or the airline miles. You could express your discontent at the situation if you really must; but is there really any doubt that your stranded-at-the-gate self is actually angry at this outcome? Nope. We all know you're unhappy. We're unhappy too.

So, what is the point of complaining? Are you actually trying to improve your situation? Or are you actually worsening your situation (worst case) or extending the amount of time you can wallow in it (best case)? Ask yourself—what do you want from the action you are about to undertake?

As professionals, we have all faced the situation when there is nothing more that we can do. We don't control the weather; we made a mistake and cannot go back in time to fix it; or maybe we simply screwed up and don't have any idea how or why. In all of these cases, you are aware that it is not good. Does someone complaining make you want to fix it more or less? Usually less.

Ask yourself before you set off to complain—what is my goal here? What am I actually hoping to get from this situation? If you want something, ask for it. If you just want to be upset, be upset. If you just want to be upset and make other people upset too, knock it off. It's not productive, and it's embarrassing. It's fine to be frustrated, upset, and angry when things don't go your way. In my office during the COVID-19 pandemic, we adopted the phrase "frustrated, but pleasant" as our office mantra. Are we frustrated when plans change again (and again)? Yes. Does complaining help? Nope. We're "frustrated, but pleasant." What's your mantra?

———————————

Adapted from original posting as *ConsumerCorner.2021.Letter.09.* (https://agribusiness.purdue.edu/consumer_corner/why-are-you -complaining/)

11

HEY, AG INDUSTRIES!

Don't Be All Hat, No Cattle

BY CAMILLE (CAMI) RYAN AND NICOLE J. OLYNK WIDMAR

Don't be all hat and no cattle when it comes to public-facing communication.

What if we told you that you were all hat, no cattle? Well, that burns, doesn't it? It insinuates that someone is all talk, can't substantiate words or claims, and is fundamentally a poser. In the agriculture and ranch world, "all hat, no cattle" is a real insult. It inflicts a wound from a place of (perceived) authority, stability, and solid ground. It insinuates that those delivering the insult are grounded, true, and righteous, while the recipient is not. It is a timeless offense, even finding its way into political discourse. It was notably used as an insult against President George W. Bush by a U.S. congresswoman in response to his 2004 State of the Union address and resurfaced in a 2019 *Washington Post* article.

"All hat, no cattle" is an ideal agriculturalist insult of an interesting flavor because, in theory, we are the ones with the cattle. We're the grounded ones—the experts, if you will. We are wholesome and hardworking—the cowboys, the legends, the pioneers, the salt-of-the-earth folks. We can't possibly be "all hat, no cattle." I'm wearing the hat, and I've got the cows.

But what if we've got it wrong? Science communication, especially public-facing science communication, is challenging—even more during a pandemic such as when COVID-19 vaccine hesitancy and misinformation threatened economic and societal recovery. If we want to walk the walk and back up our own talk, then we need to accept that responsibility lies with us—the communicators—to translate our understanding of the science.

Perhaps, more importantly, we need to thoughtfully consider that:

1. Communication is not a one-way transmission of information or indoctrination or about enhancing scientific literacy, and
2. Communication is a multifaceted exchange in which we open ourselves up to more meaningful conversations as a way to connect and learn. And, yes, accept that we will open ourselves up to criticism.

Communication is not a two-way paved highway; it's a Rocky Mountain Rangeland! Agricultural industries are awash in scientific advancements worth communicating—and worth communicating well. Society is watching. These days there is no isolated ranch life and no way to keep things off the books. We're living in a time of radical transparency when people want—actually, they demand—transparency as a way of life for industries, individual businesses, and other entities. While COVID-19 brought many societal systems to their knees, the agricultural and food supply systems, despite being under strain and increased public scrutiny, demonstrated that they were reasonably resilient.

But how committed are we to effective science communication? Agricultural industries increasingly claim to value transparency and better relationships with the general public (and not just our direct business-to-business customers or clientele). You don't simply accomplish transparency and then wash your hands and move on to the next task. Transparency is a continuous process. To operate within glass walls requires humility. The path isn't always clear, and the terrain is anything but smooth. The rangeland of public expectations is rugged and changing, scrutinized by a critical audience.

Communication means vulnerability and tradeoffs are inevitable. It's about give and take. Science communication isn't marketing. Education isn't trying to change someone's mind to agree with you. I (Nicole) recently said, "At the end of the day, you can't force people to believe something, you can't force people to want something, but we can do our best to communicate science in such a way that people can see the consequences, both positive and negative." And while this may be frustrating, it's also true. Tradeoffs are a realistic and necessary part of progress.

Communication fundamentally opens us up to criticism and exposes varying positions or viewpoints. We are all operating with incomplete information, and science is always teaching us something new or different from what we previously knew or shared.

Sharing openly and honestly is a risk, both personally and in business. True transparent, authentic communication means putting yourself out there. If you're really being transparent and honest with yourself, there will be some less-than-flattering angles to be seen alongside the social media–ready versions of our stories. It's the same hat, but different cattle and different rangeland. We can't skip the hard stuff, because the stuff we refuse to deal with today—maybe it's hard, uncomfortable, unflattering, or simply deemed less important—forms the fodder for tomorrow's misinformation. Again, transparency isn't a goal—it's a way of life. And transparency, alongside humble communication, means that we need to lean into discomfort ourselves.

In chapter 5 we discussed that words matter. "If you are serious about engaging in conversations (and not just one-sided soapbox speeches of your own making) on potential contentious issues, recognize that words matter, and mind your manners."

We posit that consensus is not required for progress:

When we set out to talk to someone on the other side of an emotionally charged issue, especially one that challenges . . . closely held moral or ethical beliefs, chances are high the conversation will end with two disagreeing parties. Even if the intention of the exchange is to explain and willingly attempt to understand what is being communicated in return, the other party may not change their views dramatically. There's no guarantee that just because someone listens and understands you, they will take to your side. (Vincent et al. 2017, 131)

Taken all together, the fundamental feature of conversation is two-way communication among willing participants with the recognition that even if you perform beautifully, the other party may simply not ever agree with you—and you may not ever agree with them. But that doesn't excuse us, the ones with the cattle, from wearing the hat well or trying on new hats for size.

WORK CITED

Vincent, Bruce, Nicole J. Olynk Widmar, and Jessica Eise. 2017. *Against the Odds: A Path Forward for Rural America.* CreateSpace Independent Publishing Platform.

_____

Adapted from original posting as *ConsumerCorner.2021.Letter.16.* (https://agribusiness.purdue.edu/consumer_corner/all-hat-no-cattle/)

12

DON'T EAT RANDOM MUSHROOMS

*C*onsumer *Corner* was originally created to bring forth consumer-derived insights drawn from nontraditional places to provide a better understanding for those in food and agricultural businesses. If you've followed the series long enough, you probably know I refer to my good friend Alice (yes, the Alice from *Alice's Adventures in Wonderland*) quite a bit. When *Consumer Corner* first began, we took to Alice to learn about what problems are worth solving (see chapter 1). On our very first half-birthday of *Consumer Corner* postings, we celebrated with inspiration from the *Alice in Wonderland* unbirthday song, which suggests that every day but one each year is an unbirthday. The point? There's always an excuse to celebrate.

Now, I know what you're thinking, because I'm thinking it too. It would simply be unjust to celebrate any *Consumer Corner* birthday without Alice, who has now become our good friend. She's seen us through a lot, and she's not done providing inspiration.

Personally, I would not suggest eating any part of a random mushroom you find, no matter how inviting the path you're on when you find it. Not even if a talking caterpillar were to explain that eating one side of the mushroom will make you grow larger, while the other side will make you smaller. Although it wasn't an issue in Lewis Carroll's 1865 novel, *Alice's Adventures in Wonderland,* or Disney's 1951 animated *Alice in Wonderland* film, one may wish to question how a round mushroom has sides anyway.

It seems the decision-making situation was dire for Alice from the start, given a round mushroom and explicit instructions about "sides." Never mind the fact that these instructions are coming from a talking caterpillar; she's about to eat a mushroom as an experiment to see which side will make her grow taller and which side will make her grow shorter anyway. But we all know how this story goes—she ate one side, and the outcome was poor. So, naturally, she ate the other side to balance it out and get herself just right. At this point, we're obligated to question the decision-making capacity of Alice, who drank the "Drink Me" blue drink, ate the "Eat Me" cookies, and experimented with eating one side of a mushroom to balance out the effects of having eaten the other side.

Sure, Alice sounds like a decision-making nightmare, yet she simultaneously sounds all too familiar. Our own decisions are often fraught with questionable paths, meandering along more like Alice than perhaps most of us care to admit. Back in chapter 1, I stated rather flippantly when introducing the decision-making capacity of Alice: "Spoiler alert: Consuming one mushroom in the forest with undesirable outcomes might make one pause before assuming that the solution to the next challenge is simply a different mushroom." Now, here we are in chapter 12, and I still think this is true. At the very least, it's reason to pause. Even better? Perhaps don't eat the random mushroom in the first place.

There are many reasons why we struggle with making decisions, particularly when we claim we're making data-driven decisions but then pause or turn back when the data doesn't align with our instincts. Perhaps the dataset is simply not large enough or doesn't cover a long enough time to offer the insights we're seeking. There are psychological decision traps, or biases inherent in our thinking or interpretation of data, and the deeply instilled preference for sticking it out and refusing to pull the plug (as discussed in chapter 7). You might remember Operation Mall Bunny, where we reminded ourselves that refusing to change one's mind is a learned skill—a challenge children certainly do not seem to have. The most fundamental challenge is this: In order to make the right choice, you must first know what you are getting into and where you are attempting to go.

"Would you tell me, please, which way I ought to go from here?"

"That depends a good deal on where you want to get to," said the Cat.

"I don't much care where—" said Alice.

"Then it doesn't matter which way you go," said the Cat.

"—so long as I get *somewhere*," Alice added as an explanation.

"Oh, you're sure to do that," said the Cat, "if you only walk long enough." (Carroll 1865, chap. 6)

THE UNFORTUNATE TRUTHS OF DATA-DRIVEN DECISIONS

Unfortunate Truth One: Data can't assist you in making a decision toward an end that you have not yet defined. You have to know where you want to go before you can hope to make decisions that get you there.

Data-driven decision-making has been a recent focus of attention by executives in businesses and even individuals in everyday life. An informed decision is certainly superior to an uninformed one. Using real-world data to make real-world decisions simply makes sense. However, there are underappreciated challenges with this approach. These challenges are numerous, but two key ones rise to the top: (1) You actually need data and analytics, and (2) you have to figure out how to actually give yourself the opportunity to do what the data tells you to do. Number two is especially hard because data-driven decisions don't mean following the data only when it aligns with what you want to do.

Unfortunate Truth Two: You can no longer do whatever you want to do, what feels right, or what your gut says to do. You may now have to do things you might not necessarily *want* to do, and that is really hard sometimes.

The House Advantage by Jeffrey Ma (2010) outlines a whole series of examples of unfortunate truth two. If you're not familiar, Jeff Ma was the real-life inspiration for the movie *21*, gaining worldwide recognition in the MIT Blackjack Club. He used math to beat the house and he says, "Every decision you make at that blackjack table is 100% objective; there is no subjectivity, the numbers are all played out. Blackjack was big data before there was even such a thing." *The House Advantage* is required reading in my Farm Management class where I pose the question: How is making a decision in blackjack—a game in which we have probabilities of various outcomes but no certainty—any different from making a decision on the farm where we also have probabilities of various outcomes but no certainty?

There are times that the math tells you to do something you don't want to do. Maybe it's making a big bet, and that's simply scary. Maybe last time you made the right decision but had a bad outcome, so this time you're feeling timid about making the right decision in the face of uncertainty.

Unfortunate Truth Three: You cannot let the fear of a bad outcome stop you from making the right decision. It is entirely possible to make the right decision and experience a bad outcome, and it's also possible to make the wrong decision and experience a good outcome. However, the outcome is not what we should be worried about in evaluating the decision. Instead, we need to separate the decision from the outcome.

From Jeff Ma:

> I'm standing behind you, let's say next year in Vegas, you have a 16 and the dealer has a 9 up. And you say to me, hey Jeff, what did you say I was supposed to do here. I say, hey, you're supposed to hit. If you get a 5 to make 21 and win, I'm a genius, but if you get a 6 to get 22 and lose, I'm a moron that they never should have made a book or a movie about. But in both cases the decision was 100% correct; one was just a poor outcome and the other was a great outcome. (Ma, https://www.youtube.com/watch?v=yKot22nCkuE, min. 5.35)

Back in chapter 1 we discussed why a raven is like a writing desk. The answer is that a raven is not like a writing desk and it doesn't matter why, but hundreds of people (probably more?) have attempted to answer this riddle, because that is what we do—try to find the answers to the questions we have.

Unfortunate Truth Four: You have to be able to identify questions that have no meaningful answers. If we're going to invest time, effort, and money into data-driven decisions, we need to prioritize which decisions are deserving of our attention. Don't chase unicorns, and don't set out to answer questions for which the answer is irrelevant.

WORKS CITED

Carroll, L. 1865. *Alice's Adventures in Wonderland.* Macmillan.

Ma, J. 2010. *The House Advantage: Playing the Odds to Win Big in Business.* St. Martin's Press.

Sharpsteen, B. (Director). (1951). *Alice in Wonderland* [Motion Picture].

Adapted from original posting as *ConsumerCorner.2021.Article.06.* (https://agribusiness.purdue.edu/consumer_corner/dont-eat-random -mushrooms/)

13

YOU (PROBABLY) DESERVED THAT

Natural consequences are often positioned to parents as things that happen to their children because they are imposed by nature, society at large, or—simply stated—any force or person except for you. I have spent a lot of time on *Consumer Corner* pointing out the failures of adults relative to children in the decision-making arena. One can ask a child for their take on shopping behavior, and the answer is straightforward and logical: "People get food for their family to eat and things that they need." And simultaneously: "It's kind of like when I was playing *Monopoly*. I saved up all my money and good cards until I really needed them or if bad stuff happened. Then if I ran out of bad cards, I could use my good cards and money for backups." Furthermore, children are much better than adults at being unafraid to assess a situation and change direction, as you might recall from Operation Mall Bunny.

Young kids are honest, sometimes to a fault. They change their minds without apology, and until we turn them on to rampant consumerism, they're actually quite reasonable consumers. They're decent at assessing tradeoffs, considering they don't possess an understanding of money, nor can they read on their own.

Then we adults introduce parenting philosophies involving natural consequences, in which we allow nature to teach a lesson to these children, who are pure in their decision-making up to this point. Natural consequences are widely appreciated and logical. But what is wrong with adults—and the businesses that we run—that we then seem unable to accept our own natural consequences? Natural consequences of being a rude coworker? Rude customer? Starring in a YouTube video about how not to act in an airport, perhaps in a scene as described in chapter 10, and now coworkers are pretending they don't know you? What about refusing to give new-customer pricing to your existing customers who are now looking elsewhere so they can be treated like a new customer? Seems like a case for natural consequences, doesn't it?

Freedom to choose and to conduct business is not freedom from the consequences of those actions, especially not if those consequences are handed down by the unforgiving market. There are three takeaways here: (1) Maintain a focus on what is important and on the primary objectives you are pursuing; (2) just because you can doesn't mean you should; and (3) freedom of choice is not freedom from consequences, natural or otherwise. Also, you probably deserved that.

Adapted from original posting as *ConsumerCorner.2021.Letter.36.* (https://agribusiness.purdue.edu/consumer_corner/you-probably -deserved-that/)

14

CONVERSATIONS

When Being Right Takes You Down the Wrong Path

BY CAMILLE (CAMI) RYAN

Our conversations about agriculture and food production frequently escalate into arguments at key moments—moments when we feel we have been aggrieved, mistreated, or wronged. We all agree that inaccurate information informs many people's perspectives about agriculture and other things like science and public health. Misinformation can shape perceptions in damaging ways. It misrepresents our industries, our livelihoods, and—yes—our way of life.

That. Gets. Personal.

When things get *personal*, or when we feel violated or wronged, things can quickly go off track in unexpected ways. We let go of any desire we may have to solve a problem or reach consensus; we lose whatever hold we have on goodwill or in building trust; and we direct our attention to an entirely different goal: being right. I've done it. You've done it. We've all done it. And here's the paradox: Those we are arguing with believe they are right, too.

THE OUTCOMES

- The minute we move into the *being right* mindset, we lose the conversation.

- When we try to impart being right onto others, we lose the relationship.

How do we avoid our very human nature to focus conversational wins and prioritize the relationship instead?

I was invited to the American Farm Bureau Convention in January 2022 to give a keynote at the "Communicate, Connect, and Influence" program. I also led a couple of breakout sessions on this very topic—having tough conversations. During the program, we all shared our experiences and our learnings.

First and foremost, we learned that a deliberate effort to let go of our need to be right helps de-escalate emotions—especially our own.

Additionally, there are some key things to consider as we have these tough conversations:

- Avoid leading with the facts. It's best to lead with a narrative or personal anecdote. Remember: Your story is the best story.
- Actively listen. Ask yourself: "Am I listening or am I reloading?" A mentor of mine once gave me very wise advice: Be present in your conversations.
- Ask questions—then ask more. This tactic helps you keep your emotions in check and really helps reduce tension in the conversation.
- "I don't know" may be the best three words to use. Follow them with: "But I will find out."
- Be accountable. If you make a mistake, admit it. If you share incorrect information, correct it. If you step out of line, acknowledge it. Apologize.
- Be human, be vulnerable. As weird as it sounds, being vulnerable and accountable for your mistakes can be personally empowering. It reveals your humanity and gives you the social license to continue to be human. Mistakes will happen. Engagement is and always will be an imperfect process.
- Finally, remember that it is a conversation, not a conversion.

What we continue to learn through the process of dialogue is that changing hearts and minds can't be our primary goal. Our conversations about agriculture should put relationships first.

It's not about keeping score. There are no end zones, no goal posts. When we begin to look at these conversations as leisurely walks down country roads instead of games, the conversations become easier and more enduring, especially when we focus on who's beside us on that road instead of what's in front or behind.

I like metaphors, so maybe another way to view these conversations is to picture them as opportunities to plant good-quality seeds about food production and sustainability in authentic ways. The key thing is that we also need to continuously steward those exchanges and relationships into the future. Our lives and livelihoods depend on it.

———————

Adapted from original posting as *ConsumerCorner.2022.Article.3*. (https://agribusiness.purdue.edu/consumer_corner/conversations-when -being-right-takes-you-down-the-wrong-path/)

15

NO

No. That's it. That's the whole title. Offended? Probably. Most of us don't react kindly to being told no. Children, at least, are honest about their displeasure at being told no. They don't like to hear no, and they make sure you know about it. Adults have much worse learned behaviors, as seen in chapter 7 when we discussed our inability to stop digging ourselves deeper instead of stopping. When told no, adults attempt to negotiate, justify, or persuade in an effort to turn that no into a yes by:

- Extending previously unmovable deadlines,
- Explaining (again) why the ask is actually not a big one, or
- Pointing out the loss of opportunities associated with this no.

Now, responses from the giver of the no could then rightfully include:

- Being (rightfully) cranky that the deadline provided was apparently unnecessary, thus proving that while you were important enough to be asked, you weren't important enough to be provided full information,
- Explaining that if this is not a big deal, then it seems like a high-pressure sales tactic being applied to a no-big-deal ask, which seems to indicate the task being asked is bigger or more consuming

than being presented. Otherwise, why is the asker expending so much effort to convince rather than just do it themselves, or
- Pointing out that the loss of opportunity may not be a loss at all—especially if simply turning down the opportunity has already proven difficult.

We know from Megan LeBoutillier's book *No Is a Complete Sentence* that *no* is a complete sentence (LeBoutillier 1995). The fact that Megan LeBoutillier had to write a book about it would suggest that perhaps we know, but we don't really know. There are a lot of sayings intended to help us say no, but it seems we have not internalized them. We have lots of advice to help us remember tradeoffs. "When everything is a priority, then nothing is a priority." "Saying yes to something is saying no to something else."

Saying no is really important for our own productivity, in work and in life. Note that there is a difference between being busy and being productive. You can say yes to everything and be extremely busy, but are you actually productive in anything (or happy for that matter)? In her article "This Is Why Saying 'No' Is the Best Way to Grow Your Career—and How to Do It," Amy Blaschka references billionaire Warren Buffett's philosophy: "The difference between successful people and really successful people is that really successful people say no to almost everything" (Blaschka 2019).

Certainly, the business and leadership worlds have coalesced around the notion that no is important. Yet, we continue to struggle. So, ask yourself:

- If this isn't a big ask and isn't a big deal, why are you being asked to do it?
- More importantly, why do we struggle so much to say no to such a great opportunity?

WORKS CITED

Blaschka, A. 2019, November 26. "This Is Why Saying 'No' Is the Best Way to Grow Your Career—And How to Do It." Retrieved from forbes.com:

https://www.forbes.com/sites/amyblaschka/2019/11/26/this-is-why
-saying-no-is-the-best-way-to-grow-your-career-and-how-to-do-it/?sh=66
43a681479d.

LeBoutillier, M. 1995. *"No" Is a Complete Sentence*. Ballantine Books.

_____

Adapted from original posting as *ConsumerCorner.2022.Letter.9*
(https://agribusiness.purdue.edu/consumer_corner/no/)

16

THE QUEEN AND I

What I Learned About Leadership
from the Honeybees

BY COURTNEY BIR

This year, I was challenged to think about leadership. Swarming, for bees, is a natural process during which some members of the hive leave with the original queen to find a new home. The bees that are left raise a new queen and keep on going with their bee lives. The swarm flies around resting in different places while scouts go look for a new home. The cost of bees has increased; purchasing bees from another beekeeper can range from $100 to $270. At those prices, it becomes clear why beekeepers are interested in catching these swarms of free bees looking for a new home, even if they have unknown origins, genetics, and temperament.

I caught several swarms of bees in the tree in my front yard last summer. I kept one of these swarms and established a new hive. Going into fall, I felt good about my new, free-to-me bees living happily in their pink (and stylish) hive. They seemed gentle enough and were off to a good start. Both of my hives made it through the winter, and I was hopeful for a honey-filled summer. As an economist, I should have known there is no such thing as a free lunch.

When I opened the hives this spring, I quickly realized the swarm hive was very, very aggressive. I was stung through my suit fifteen times, and my poor husband (who has been dragged into this hobby) was stung seventeen times. Bees sometimes do not show their true nature until they have resources to protect. Since they were from unknown stock, their fall be-havior wouldn't necessarily last as the population grew. We needed a plan.

There are three types of bees: the queen (there is only one), workers (all female and the bulk of the population), and drones (males). Fun fact about male bees—they do absolutely no work in the hive. Their only pur-pose is to go out and breed virgin queens. Going into winter, the females literally throw the baby boys out of the hive to save food, but I digress; all workers and drones are the sons and daughters of the queen. The queen's genetics, which determine attitude, affect the entire hive.

To state it simply: I had a mean queen, so I had a mean hive of bees. The answer to my problem was to replace the evil queen with a gentler queen with known genetics and wait. After a couple of months, the majority of the evil queen's offspring would have lived their life, leaving only the gen-tle offspring of the new queen. After just two weeks, I was shocked at the behavior of the bees. They were still aggressive, but they were not angrily flying at my face. The new queen was already changing the behavior of the bees through her pheromones. I will admit, the aggressive bees were ex-tremely productive. There's an old wives' tale among beekeepers that ag-gressive bees make more honey. But at what cost?

This whole experience has made me think about leadership among hu-mans, not just in bee colonies. Can the leader's bad attitude shape the en-tire culture of the group? Even if the group is being productive, is the atti-tude destroying relationships and hurting you in the long run? I replaced a productive but destructive leader to improve my long-term success (and stay in the good graces of my neighbors). It may not be as cut and dried in your organization, and interventions like training or discussions can be helpful. But for me and my evil queen (bee, that is), the only answer was off with her head!

Adapted from original posting as *ConsumerCorner.2022.Letter.22.* (https://agribusiness.purdue.edu/consumer_corner/the-queen-and-me -what-i-learned-about-leadership-from-the-honeybees/)

17

SHADES OF GRAY

Most of the pivotal aspects of what we do in life can be boiled down to the decisions we make—big ones that shape the paths of future possibilities or little ones that stack up to become who we are or how we behave.

Most of the time, though, the answer to our decisions is: It depends. Should we be transparent with our consumers? Generally, yes—but make sure people are asking and be sure you aren't just sharing for your benefit instead of theirs. Now that I think about it, I guess the answer to that question can also be bluntly put: It depends. In chapter 15, we asked why we have such a hard time saying no to people. Well, we have a deep-seated fear of missing out, and we want people to like us or at least not give them a reason to dislike us. But taking on too much is a decision we make. It isn't simple, and there is not a right and a wrong answer. Again, it depends.

Chapter 13 explored the idea that we like to think people get what they deserve—we let children experience the natural consequences of their behavior but are shocked (and angry) when we experience them ourselves. Perhaps it is because we know that life isn't fair. You do not always get what you deserve, and neither does that other guy. It's also entirely possible (actually, inevitable) that you'll make a decision that is 100 percent correct but still suffer a poor outcome (remember chapter 12?). Worse yet, it's also inevitable that you will make a decision that is patently wrong but experience success. This is dangerous. At best, you learned nothing. At worst, you learned that doing the wrong thing paid off.

We could lament at great lengths the challenges associated with decision-making itself, but relatively little attention is given to exploring alternatives, options, or outcomes. Is it really a win or lose situation? Is it black and white, or are there shades of gray? In my own class, I propose that very few (if any) decisions leave us with no alternatives, forcing us to accept the status quo or only a single option. I further propose that there are very few decisions that we face for which there are only two choices—most of the time, we can think creatively to craft a whole suite of options. Arguably, the shades of gray associated with a question are related to where you fit into the situation: "When you're the victim of the behavior, it's black and white; when you're the perpetrator, there are a million shades of gray" (Dr. Laura Schlessinger).

But, then again, there are a few situations—not many, but a few—for which there is one way or the other with no wiggle room. As the sayings go, you cannot be a little bit pregnant or a little bit married. You are either married or you are not. The same applies to games with known and accepted rulebooks: "It's about you. If you win, it's you; if you lose, it's you. Black and white. Nowhere to hide" (Greg Rusedski).

The catch in our daily lives is that we do not have known and accepted rulebooks. Even in the most structured of business environments and in the legal arena, there are creative ways to structure deals or new contracts to be developed. Now, at some point you may find yourself facing a judgment, whether in life or legally, in which the ultimate answer will be determined on a given matter. But that happens in an extremely small share of situations. Most of the time, we have negotiations, and we arrive at some middle place between one extreme and the other, or shall we say, we arrive at a shade of gray. One party's perspective may differ from another's, and most situations are wide open for creative problem-solving and many, many shades of gray.

Adapted from original posting as *ConsumerCorner.2022.Letter.48*. (https://agribusiness.purdue.edu/consumer_corner/shades-of-gray/)

18

SQUIRRELS ARE
BETTER THAN PEOPLE

Inspired by Sundaram et al. (2018).

S quirrels are better than people—at least when it comes to
decision-making. They're rational and consistent, even though they
may appear somewhat haphazard when playing in traffic. (I said
they were rational as consumers; I didn't say they were geniuses.)

Unlike squirrels, human consumers vary their tastes and preferences,
plus individuals are fickle and inconsistent, even internally. Case in point:
Chocolate is my favorite, but today I want vanilla. Chocolate is still my
favorite, but when I see both options side by side ... hmm, I don't know
which one I want. My favorite is available—it's right there. But wait, what
is that new, unknown flavor over there? Should I try that instead?

Squirrels, in contrast, are incredibly consistent. In our studies, we found
no measurable heterogeneity in consumer tastes or preferences among
squirrels. They sometimes selected different things, but they were the correct things for that squirrel in that time and place, and it didn't vary across
squirrels. Squirrels are unbelievably consistent food shoppers. In fact, they
shop properly for eating versus storing (caching) and for the time of year.

Squirrels are model shoppers, selecting the right thing for their needs at the right time. I was fortunate to be able to work on a project looking at squirrels as consumers. It was a project led out of the lab of Robert Swihart in Purdue University's Department of Forestry and Natural Resources, and in collaboration with Nathanael Lichti and Mekala Sundaram (who were both affiliated with Purdue University's Department of Forestry and Natural Resources at the time). Essentially, we were looking at how squirrels made decisions. Squirrels, like many animals, are rational out of necessity. They need to figure out how to feed themselves with some degree of competence in order to survive. In contrast, human consumer tastes and preferences are unpredictable. What we like today might not be what we like tomorrow, and we choose to buy more or less of available items according to our own whims, in additional to budgetary and food availability constraints. Squirrels may be impacted by what is available to select among, but they're incredibly consistent in what they're selecting (not like us humans).

WORK CITED

Sundaram, Mekala, Nathanael Lichti, Nicole J. Olynk Widmar, and Robert Swihart. 2018. "Eastern Gray Squirrels Are Consistent Shoppers of Seed Traits: Insights from Discrete Choice Experiments." *Integrative Zoology* 280–96.

Adapted from original posting as *ConsumerCorner.2023.Letter.05.* (https://agribusiness.purdue.edu/consumer_corner/squirrels-are-better -than-people/)

19

SMELL YOUR
CHEESE TO SEE
IF IT'S GETTING OLD

At *Consumer Corner*, we have a long—and admittedly odd—history of learning from rodents. Back in chapter 4, we explored why we relate so closely to animals, even the rodent-like ones, from an early age. Of course, it isn't only rodents—we also connect with bears, dolphins, cats, and so, so, so many dogs.

Now, back to rodents. Even Mickey Mouse, for all his beloved status, still has some unattractive traits. He's an icon, a childhood dream, an economic powerhouse—but at the end of the day, he's still a rodent. A rodent with tiny paws that we cover up with big white gloves. From Mickey's gloves, we learn to question transparency and uncomfortable truths. Who are we really being transparent for? Is it to benefit our consumers and address their concerns? Or, if not, then why?

In our enthusiasm for the famous rodents, we may have missed a more basic lesson from regular, less famous mice. You may have read *Who Moved My Cheese?* by Spencer Johnson (1998). If you haven't, you should. And if it's been a while, it's worth a refresher.

The book follows two little people, Hem and Haw, and two mice, Sniff and Scurry, through a maze. Everyone wants to find cheese, which seemingly represents success more broadly defined than a stash of physical product. The cheese is the embodiment of success, whatever that means in your vision.

The bottom line is this: Hem and Haw (with all their human problems) search for cheese by overthinking, emotionalizing, and attaching meaning to the outcome before they've even found it. Sniff and Scurry (with none of the human problems) just go. Their motivation is simple: "We want cheese. We are hungry." The first lesson? Stop complicating matters with how you will feel once you find the cheese and what it means to you. Start looking for cheese and get going.

The second lesson imparts a vital truth: Finding success (your cheese) doesn't equate to a lifetime of entitlement to cheese. If you become too fixated on your hard-found cheese, you may not notice when the pile begins shrinking and growing mold. Essentially, if you stop looking, stop paying attention, and become engrossed with your pile of cheese, you might not notice when it starts to stink. You must smell your cheese often. Finding success is not a one-and-done sort of thing. It's constant. In the story, the mice keep their sneakers handy, so they are ready to run. You need to keep your sneakers close. When the cheese gets old, pay attention, and then set out to find new cheese.

Instead of fixating on having found cheese and parking oneself next to said pile, Sniff and Scurry (the mice) move on easily and run after new cheese. Hem and Haw (human problems, again) feel sad and sorrowful about their moldy, tiny cheese pile. The longer you stand next to your sadness-inducing moldy cheese crumbles, the less time you have to find new cheese. At some point the fear of leaving the old cheese becomes crippling. Eventually, Haw goes out to find new cheese without his human friend Hem. But it took a lot to get him to go, and they aren't together anymore. There's new cheese out there, but you aren't going to find it standing next to your old moldiness. Smell your cheese so you know when it is getting old. Then . . . Go. Find. New. Cheese. Preferably without too much Hemming and Hawing.

WORKS CITED

Johnson, Spencer. 1998. *Who Moved My Cheese?* Putnam Adult.

Seuss, Dr. 1957. *The Cat in the Hat*. Random House, Houghton Mifflin.

Vincent, Bruce, Nicole J. Olynk Widmar, and Jessica Eise. 2017. *Against the Odds: A Path Forward for Rural America*. CreateSpace Independent Publishing Platform.

White, E. B. 1945. *Stuart Little*. Harper & Brothers.

White, E. B. 1952. *Charlotte's Web*. Harper & Brothers.

Adapted from original posting as *ConsumerCorner.2023.Letter.13*. (https://agribusiness.purdue.edu/consumer_corner/smell-your-cheese-to-see-if-it-is-getting-old/)

20

CHANGE IS NOT ALWAYS BAD

---

s the wise Sheldon Cooper once said in *The Big Bang Theory* (Season 2, Episode 19), "Change is never fine. They say it is, but it's not." He goes on to share various thoughts about change over the years, generally circling around a distaste for it or an overall feeling of being overwhelmed. After all, this was a man who once said, "I've spent my whole life trying to bring order to the universe by carefully planning every moment of every day."

Indeed, some of us (speaking for myself here) like order—lists, calendars, planning, and then a little extra planning just to be sure. Spontaneity has never been my strong suit, unless you mean explicitly scheduling time for unstructured or free time, in which case I absolutely do excel. Calendars, lists, rules (especially rules); I'm good at those. Now, when it comes to change, preferably well-planned change, I'm trying really hard. Recall from chapter 19 in which we talked about the book *Who Moved My Cheese?* by Spencer Johnson (1998). I summarized:

> Instead of fixating on having found cheese and parking oneself next to said pile, Sniff and Scurry (the mice) move on easily and run after new cheese. Hem and Haw (human problems, again) feel sad and sorrowful

about their moldy, tiny cheese pile. The longer you stand next to your sadness-inducing moldy cheese crumbles, the less time you have to find new cheese. At some point the fear of leaving the old cheese becomes crippling. Eventually Haw goes out to find new cheese without his human friend Hem. But it took a lot to get him to go, and they aren't together anymore. There's new cheese out there, but you aren't going to find it standing next to your old moldiness. Smell your cheese so you know when it is getting old. Then . . . Go. Find. New. Cheese. Preferably without too much Hemming and Hawing.

It makes good sense that when your cheese crumbles are covered in mold, you should move on to find some new cheese. Even though it sounds obvious, it is indeed easier said than actually done. We're using rodents to illustrate a point here—you know you need to do something different, find something different, or just *do something*. And yet, we struggle. Change is hard. And, much like our old friend Alice (in Wonderland, that is), "I give myself very good advice," and yet I'm still struggling to follow it.

Interestingly, one of Sheldon's commonly quoted idols, Albert Einstein, once said something that likely would have greatly distressed Sheldon: "The measure of intelligence is the ability to change."

Nobody cares if you are good at it. Change is inevitable. In fact, the one constant, as they say, is change. (Not that we stop to ask who *they* are, but that's a question for a different book.)

I suppose I can agree that change is not always bad.

WORK CITED

"The Dead Hooker Juxtaposition." *The Big Bang Theory*, created by Chuck Lorre and Bill Prady. Season 2, Episode 19.

Adapted from original posting as *ConsumerCorner.2023.Letter.15*. (https://agribusiness.purdue.edu/consumer_corner/change-is-not -always-bad/)

21

RESOLUTION
VS. FRUSTRATION

The Art and Absurdity of Complaining

C omplaints are unpleasant. We cringe at the prospect of someone complaining—especially when we're on the receiving end. The reality is that we often cringe when watching others do it too, even when we're mostly uninvolved and not related to the person doing it loudly in public and for everyone to stare at.

But why? Why are you complaining?

Maybe you are seeking a resolution to your problem or concern. It's plausible that you genuinely want a resolution. In such a case, you want to evoke change or seek a remedy. If you received a pizza covered in anchovies despite explicitly and repeatedly saying, "No anchovies," couldn't you simply ask the person for the correct pizza? And perhaps you should stop to consider whether repeatedly saying *anchovies* over and over while ordering might have contributed to the outcome. You could complain, whine, and yell at someone about your fish-meets-pizza issues. Or, if your true desire is a plain pizza with no anchovies, you could straightforwardly ask for one and skip scolding the person who made it incorrectly. This is one way to address the issue: Correct the error or find a remedy.

On the flip side, maybe you want something that's entirely beyond reach. Your flight out of Miami is canceled due to a storm. We've all witnessed, or perhaps even been there ourselves a time or two, this type of airport-induced hissy fit. Despite the fact it's not the gate agent's fault, they graciously bear the brunt of said hissy fit.

What's the objective here?

Why direct complaints toward the gate agent who, inevitably, lacks control over the destiny of this aircraft? Does your public display of frustration make the plane fly? Will it change the meteorologist's mind? Do you even really want that to happen? Complaining so loudly that eventually someone relents and allows you to board a plane for a destination deemed unsafe or unacceptable three minutes earlier doesn't seem like much of a win. Venting might make you feel better, but it sure won't make that hurricane change its course. Sure, you might earn a hotline to someone higher up or in customer service. But seriously, is that your endgame? Last I checked you wanted to get the heck out of Miami.

Perhaps you're on the quest for restitution. Miles, a free hotel room, or even a heartfelt apology are on your wish list. Indeed, you might be entitled to such perks, provided you haven't turned your complaint into a cringe-worthy YouTube scene. But let's be real—complaining isn't the only path here. It's not the smoothest journey for the complainer or the target of those complaints. You could ask for the perks or express your discontent, but let's not pretend your hurricane-induced theatrics aren't just a thinly veiled tantrum about the inevitable outcome. We get it; you're not thrilled. Spoiler alert: Neither are we.

Why are you complaining—to improve the situation? Chances are you might be making things worse. What do you want out of this activity?

We've all encountered situations like this as professionals when there is nothing left to do. We don't control the weather. We can't reverse our mistakes, or maybe we screwed up and don't know how or why. At any rate, we're aware it's not a good situation. Was it that colleague complaining that made you want to fix it? Often, the answer is no.

As frustrated as you might be, your words—what you say and how you say it—do matter (as we discussed in chapter 5). Before you decide to take flight on a complaining spree, ask yourself: Where do I hope to land? What do I really hope to get out of this situation? If it's something specific, articulate it. If you just want to wallow in frustration, go ahead. However, if you want to be angry and take it out on others, knock it off. It's unproductive and embarrassing.

———————

Adapted from original posting as *ConsumerCorner.2023.Letter.23.* (https://agribusiness.purdue.edu/consumer_corner/resolution-vs -frustration-the-art-and-absurdity-of-complaining/)

22

AUTHENTICITY OVER PLASTIC PERFECTION

As we scroll through social media and see curated highlight reels from the lives of our acquaintances, it's easy to overlook the imperfections that linger beneath the surface of their perfect lives. Do we find ourselves comparing or momentarily feeling inadequate? Sure. Claiming otherwise is like saying your attempt at that perfect selfie wasn't followed by twenty retakes and a blur filter.

Flawless lives are about as real as Barbie's résumé—endless careers, no bad hair days, and a dream house that defies all logic. Let's be real: No one is out there living their best life every day. The mixed feelings about Barbie reflect reality: Some love her, some vandalize her, and the rest of us are just eye-rolling in between. After all, she's just a molded piece of plastic trying to be every girl's idol and best friend. Come on, get over yourself; no one can be that perfect, and frankly, no one wants you to be.

People aren't perfect, and brands aren't either.

There is little upside to perfectionism, both for individuals and brands. Fixating on the fear of making mistakes, disappointing others, or adhering to unrealistically high standards often leads to negative consequences. Fixation on perfection can lead to covering up mistakes instead of acknowledging them, apologizing, and doing better in the future. There's a reason you feel unsettled and skeptical when something is *too* perfect. You know it's not perfect, so the appearance of perfection makes you (rightfully) worried that you may have yet to uncover the flaw. Even worse, if there's a flaw that's so important to hide, then it must be a really bad one, right?

What makes you distinct (cringe and all) is most likely your greatest asset. Figuring that out is key to building authentic connections. Everyone is not your target audience. Revealing your strengths (and embracing your weaknesses) is an important step in truly connecting with your best customers.

Now, let's draw a marketing lesson from *Barbie*, the biggest movie of the summer of 2023. With over $1.4 billion in gross ticket sales and its global success, the movie stands as a testament to the potential of a well-crafted marketing strategy—one that reshapes stereotypes of Barbie after six decades. The key takeaway? Authenticity is paramount, even if it means a little reinvention.

Stop trying to be everything to everyone.

You might think that anyone who expresses interest in your brand is someone you should target, but this will lead you to waste time and resources on empty leads. When you attempt to be everything to everybody, you end up being someone you're not (and might not even be proud of). In the end, you lose connections and become hard to understand.

If genuine connections are what you're after, embrace your originality, own the cringe, and just be yourself. Because, in the end, authenticity is the superpower that sets you apart.

Adapted from original posting as *ConsumerCorner.2023.Letter.24.* (https://agribusiness.purdue.edu/consumer_corner/authenticity-over -plastic-perfection/)

23

LIAR, LIAR

As the saying goes, "Liar, liar, pants on fire!" Except your pants never burst into flames—at least not in response to you lying—so it turns out that was a lie too!

In chapter 3, we talked how you were a hypocrite. And you absolutely still are (sorry to be the one to tell you). In chapter 10, we talked about your YouTube-worthy temper tantrums and why they need to stop (you embarrassed yourself). Now, you're being called a liar. It's more like, "You're also a liar," implying either that you are multiple things, or that you aren't alone and we're liars too. Human behavior is a complicated thing; it's not just you.

Surveys are valuable in designing questions about specific topics, but survey data has challenges—from ensuring an adequate sample size to conduct the analyses desired, to worrying about response bias, enumerator bias, and a whole slew of other biases when we're asking questions of people. Respondents know their answers are being recorded (even if anonymously) and analyzed by other people.

Online and social media data are, in my opinion, the new frontier of data. They exist in a variety of forms, from talking on Twitter (now X) about holiday plans to images and even data collected from smart devices in your home. Social media data has been analyzed to explore public understanding of public health crises, like Zika virus, and to question whether natural disasters with more social and online media posts receive more aid or funding (spoiler: they do not). But social media has its challenges too. You post only your best life online, you might say things that are not entirely accurate, and not everyone is represented. In short, there are challenges for any dataset.

However, there is an online dataset that knows more about us than social media could ever hope to. It's that little bar into which we type our deepest secrets—even the really, really unflattering stuff, the kind that would (and should) make other people recoil if they could link it back to us. It's the Google search bar. And the resulting Google search data.

Seth Stephens-Davidowitz's book *Everybody Lies: Big Data, New Data, and What the Internet Can Tell Us About Who We Really Are* delves into a variety of topics using Google search data. People tell Google things they might not tell anyone else—not their friends, their spouse, or their doctor. Stephens-Davidowitz also posits, and I think I agree, that search data may reveal lies we even tell ourselves. So, it isn't just that we lie to others; we lie to ourselves too (Stephens-Davidowitz, 2017). Considering how much better Google search data reflects reality in the topics explored in the book compared to survey data or other more traditional data sources, it seems that we're not as prone to lying to Google (or at least not nearly as much).

Everybody Lies is presented in three parts: part I, "Data, Big and Small"; part II, "The Powers of Big Data"; and part III, "Big Data: Handle with Care." The conclusion is aptly titled "How Many People Finish Books" and suggests the answer is not very many. But it is well done and worth the read.

In *Everybody Lies*, chapter 8, "Mo Data, Mo Problems? What We Shouldn't Do," starts with the statement, "Sometimes, the power of Big Data is so impressive it's scary. It raises ethical questions." Stephens-Davidowitz argues that there is danger in empowered corporations, essentially fueled by big data, understanding who is likely to do what or determining how much a customer is willing to pay. On page 265, he writes:

> Data on the internet, in other words, can tell businesses which customers to avoid and which they can exploit. It can also tell customers the businesses they should avoid and who is trying to exploit them. Big

Data to date has helped both sides in the struggle between consumers and corporations. We have to make sure it remains a fair fight.

Just because everyone does it, doesn't make it good or right. Does everyone (or supposedly everyone) knowing something make it right? The answer: It doesn't. There are many reasons we lie or fail to share our true selves, but there are also many reasons to fight that urge to cover up or gloss over our less-than-admirable behaviors, traits, or flaws. Recall from chapter 22, "Authenticity Over Plastic Perfection," "If genuine connections are what you're after, embrace your originality, own the cringe, and just be yourself. Because, in the end, that authenticity is the superpower that sets you apart."

WORK CITED

Stephens-Davidowitz, S. (2017). *Everybody Lies: Big Data, New Data, and What the Internet Can Tell Us About Who We Really Are.* Dey Street Books.

Adapted from original posting as *ConsumerCorner.2023.Letter.25.* (https://agribusiness.purdue.edu/consumer_corner/liar-liar/)

CONCLUSION

Food and agribusiness supply chains are complex, involving a number of businesses from farm to processor to retailer, as well as input and service providers for every segment along the way. These supply chains come together to produce goods that become consumer products. Regardless of your place along the agribusiness supply chain, one topic remains universal in importance—the end product must eventually reach consumers. Throughout this process many aspects of business have a tendency to get blamed on the mythical consumer. How often have we heard or said, "The consumer needs to be educated"? Nobody wants to be forcibly educated, and forcibly educating others about the product you are trying to sell them is inherently off-putting. Instead, we should work to understand consumer desires and determine how to better meet these demands. Recognizing consumer needs and working to fulfill them is different from telling them what they need. The distinction may be subtle at first but makes a world of difference.

Perhaps more interesting, and more central to this book—and the additional books to follow in the *Consumer Corner* series—is not what we can learn about consumers but rather what we can learn from them. This volume has explored decidedly nontraditional insights into decision-making and management. The next books to follow in the series will tackle novel data, evolving data uses, market insights, developing and building resilience, and, finally, we will be rethinking everything (maybe not everything, just most things). After all, consumers are fickle, they're demanding, they're (seemingly) uninformed—they're you.

ABOUT THE AUTHORS

Nicole J. Olynk Widmar is an agricultural economist specializing in farm businesses and consumer decision-making under uncertainty. She serves as a professor and the head of the Department of Agricultural Economics at Purdue University.

Michael L. Smith is a research scientist specializing in the human dimensions of resource use, applying cross-disciplinary methods in agricultural economics and the social sciences. He works in Purdue University's Department of Agricultural Economics.

Erin Robinson is a communications and marketing professional with experience in agricultural business and academic research environments. As marketing manager for Purdue University's Center for Food and Agricultural Business, she develops marketing strategies, creates content and outreach initiatives, drives brand awareness, and evaluates marketing effectiveness.

ABOUT THE CONTRIBUTORS

Courtney Bir, assistant professor of Agricultural Economics at Oklahoma State University, holds a PhD from Purdue and master's and bachelor's degrees from OSU. Her research examines consumer preferences for agricultural products and production economics, aiming to align preferences with profitability. Her extension work focuses on farm finance and operational goal achievement.

Mario Ortez was born into a family of coffee growers in northern Nicaragua, where he first experienced agriculture. His career spans various segments of agrifood, bridging roles in the private sector and academia. Currently, he is a faculty member at Virginia Tech, dedicated to inspiring the next generation of agribusiness leaders.

Camille (Cami) Ryan, BComm, PhD, is a Bayer Science Fellow, a Professional Affiliate with the College of Agriculture at the University of Saskatchewan, and Senior Business Partner for Industry Affairs and Sustainability with Bayer CropScience Canada. With a broad academic and professional background in social sciences and economics, Ryan passionately advocates for policy based on science-based evidence in the agriculture industry.